Hotel Domilocos

D1235689

Hotel Domilocos

POEMS

Ellen Waterston

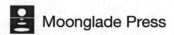 Moonglade Press

Grateful acknowledgement to the following publications where some of these poems first appeared: *Crazy Woman Creek, Constellation, Cold Snap, I Am Madagascar, Landscape: Views from Within and Beyond Creating: A Climate of Change, Fishtrap Anthology, Oregon East, Orlo's Bear Deluxe, Sagebrush Legacy, The Church by the Town Beach, The Source Weekly, Travel Oregon,* and *Vía Láctea, A Woman of a Certain Age Walks the Camino.*

Special thanks to poet Eleanor Berry for her invaluable help in shaping this book. Thanks also to Marjorie Meret Carmen for her support and encouragement, Louise Hawker for her assistance in getting *Hotel Domilocos* across the finish line, Thomas Osborne for his skills in concept and design. Thanks to Skyhooks Poets: Carol Barrett, Marion Davidson, Kake Huck, John Martin, Judith Montgomery, and Jane Thielsen for their discerning input on so many of these poems and to Jimmy Santiago-Baca, Eleanor Berry, John Calderazzo, and Bill Siverly for their generous comments about *Hotel Domilocos.* Finally, in gratitude to Playa at Summer Lake where many of these poems were written, and the Oregon Arts Commission for its support.

MOONGLADE PRESS publisher of uncommon books
Distributed by IngramSpark
Also available from:
www.moongladepress.com
www.writingranch.com

ISBN: 978-0-9987639-0-3
Library of Congress Control Number: 2017903171

PRINTED IN THE U.S.A.
FIRST EDITION/FIRST PRINTING

To Marjorie

Contents

1 HOTEL DOMILOCOS

2   Hotel Domilocos
4   Ferry to San Juan
5   Board Game
6   Lures
8   Run, Run
9   Curlicued
10 Bigger Idea
11 *Parque de Reptilandia*
12 Big Island Triptych
13 Impressions
14 Fisherman's Beach: A Requiem

II SCALE HOUSE

18 Scale House
19 Red Flag
20 Him and Carl
21 Untitled
22 Rose, A Retrospective
24 Consultation Over a Chew
25 Chicken Slaughter
26 Afternoon Light
27 Rancher Gets Metaphysical
28 Fall Desert Blooms Yellow
29 Desert Keep
30 Nowhere Called Home
31 Night Hawk
32 Another Round
33 Loudest Sounds
34 Fly Already
35 Mothering-up
36 Skin-Walker
38 Palindrome
39 Full Attention

III JAMESTOWN BRIDGE

42 Jamestown Bridge
43 Entering the Boys' School
    Dining Hall
44 Townie
45 Snack Mix
46 Stare Down
47 Closer
48 Birthday Bouquet
49 Mud Puddle Tavern
50 The Philatelist and Penny Black
52 Mr. Las Vegas
53 Summer Psalm
54 Ladies Room During
    Intermission at the Opera
55 Cat on the Window Seat
56 Kitchen Axe
57 Spider in the Sink
58 Aunt Joy to Dinner
59 Undoing

IV THE NEXT TO LAST QUESTION

62 Picto-Prayers
63 One Sudden Afternoon
64 Summer Lake in Spring
65 Datebook
66 Quick Distance
67 Mutual Creation Society
68 Pinhole
69 Dream Catcher
70 True Happenings
72 Anaconda Copper
73 American Made
74 Seiner's Dream
75 Sweet Happenstance
76 New Frontier
77 Higher Still
78 Jump Rope
79 The Next to Last Question

I

Hotel Domilocos

Hotel Domilocos

I

If wisdom springs from terrible loss, I have no use
for wisdom, Vicente cries. He weeps each time
he takes Gloria in his arms. Each time she weeps too,
her tired body all she has to soothe his despair
since the *gringo* developer plowed their shacks
under. Belongings in twined bundles, they
waited by the road, later dropped at a quick-
built slum deep in the jungle. Years pass inside
the airless box far from their fruit trees, gardens,
and sea breezes. The *gringo's* sullied touch seeps
into their coffee, tamales, bed...and the dreams
of their silk-skinned, teenage daughter. She watches
the Monarchs turn the Oyamel tree a fluttering, excited
orange, hears her parents' sighs of despair, and through
the curtain whispers to them, "I am leaving."

II

Before dinner, the guests at the Hotel Domilocos
sit in the thick darkness, staring silently at the long
and short of their lives. A German woman fans herself
with her *revista*; a lepidopterist dons a t-shirt that says
Monarch; the developer, leather-skinned from too much
smoking and sin, waits elbow-to-knee for the silk-skinned
girl he hired in the barrio. He recalls all the sultry places
he'd bought sex, the aphrodisiacs: suck the yolk from an egg
with a straw then open it and eat the chick whole or drink
snake blood. The bell rings. They all descend to dinner, move
their tables together, sit their stories side-by-side until
they blend into something better, the good eclipsing
the bad. In unison they dab sweat off their faces with white
linen napkins, in love suddenly and completely as newfound
residents of the same, blended fiction, as actors living
passionately into an accidental script, drifting toward
the last act, when the set is struck, the lights go out.

III

The girl stops outside the Hotel Domilocos, listens
to the wine-soaked laughter, sees the colored
garlands of gaiety, the smoke-stained man
who bought her. On her way there she'd happened
on the confetti trail of the Monarchs' broken wings
turning to powder in the setting sun, an orange
and black chalk line leading to somewhere
else. She overhears the butterfly man: "Never
pick up the bright fragments. Their frail scent maps
the butterflies' way to their fruit trees, gardens
and sea breezes." She turns and walks quickly
toward home.

Ferry to San Juan

The day is rude in its sunny cheer, the egrets
inconsiderate in their grace. Particularly given
Eguaro, pale from thirteen years of making friends
with pain, pain meaning at least he still has the wasted
limb. Most assume the crutches show he's on
the mend from something broken.

Eguaro waits in line for the ferry to San Juan with his
little sister. Addled as an infant from a bout with pneumonia
she rocks, wrings her hands, and in a voice thin as paper
singsongs, "*Ola, ola.*" Papa stays home, pretending
the truck needs fixing. To the mother, Flori, all this
is nothing

more than more. She has suffered her husband's fingers
severed by the ferry cable. Her brother drowned. Her sister
dead from ciguatera. The God she prays to, she has decided,
is deaf or busy. Flori earns money cutting roosters out of plastic
milk jugs, spray painting the jagged feathers orange and red.
"How quaint!" the tourists exclaim, and buy them at the galleria.

The all aboard whistle sounds. Flori walks ahead of her children
across the ramp onto the Isabella. Nothing about her demeanor
suggests that today she goes to San Juan with her son, her angel
boy, the one to be the fourth generation of ferrymen, on his last
boat ride with two legs. The egrets, wings outstretched,
turn back to shore.

Board Game

I go first, draw a country card: U.S.A. Striving. Success.
My son's turn: Costa Rica. *Pura Vida.* Do less.
Me again: Bonus for cellphone, planning calendar, ambition,
stress. My son picks. No tick, no clock, no reason to move
past square one. *But even,* I worry, *if you have a wife and children?*

Just shy of home-free, of my white bread, all-American, small town
of milk and money, I get stuck for what seems an eternity in my son's
barrio. There, moon tides salt-lick the dirt street, young men spar
to stave off boredom, human waste flows into the ocean.

At the *tienda,* government signs warn of something worse
than dengue or chikungunya. A sheet of pocked tin protects
Lita's tables from the rain. Scribbled on a paper plate,
stuck on a stick: "*Plato del Dia: Camarones.*" "You'll see,
someone will happen in," she tells her crippled daughter
who waits in a wheel-less chair. "It's our turn to get lucky."

Down the street Josafat swings a yelping mutt by the ears
for fun. Alma, next door, is young to be a grandmother,
but is. She makes coconut sorbet to sell, finds a rabbit's
paw for her altar, the guarantee of a better draw.

Swinging in a hammock of braided butterfly vines, toucans
happy-sad chuckling in the humid canopy above, my sons watches
his children skip between close-by generations of family, tend
to their pet monkey, swing on a rope over the waterfall's emerald pool
and let go. He plucks a yellow passion fruit from a tree, listens
to my endless attitude of right, pauses between bites to say, "How little
is enough, how plentiful so little can be. I love my family. I like it here.
You think your game is the better plan? If winning is the object, I win."

Lures

The night before a week of guided fishing, the men from big American cities settle in their hotel rooms at Bahia de los Muertos. Rebar sprouts from the roof. The shower drain gurgles when they flush the toilet. The electric lights shiver on and off. But there's no place they would rather be. Hunting the sea. Men among men. They gather in the front room and pass around a bottle of Tapatio, lay naked Barbies on their backs on the tile counter, and, with a kitchen knife, hack off the blonde tresses to use in tying elaborate salt water fishing lures. The butched dolls are tossed in the trash. In the morning, local kids find them. The brown girls draw clothes on the white bodies. The brown boys place small kisses on the nipple-less breasts.

Mike cinches the last lure, the hook snagging his thumb. He isn't paying attention— he's watching the young Consuela. This gringo guide has been bringing groups here for years, has witnessed Consuela come of age under her t-shirt that says "Hola Cola". What a helper to her father, Poncho, the panga captain. She cleans the fish, cooks for the guests, teaches her father the English she taught herself. What a waste, Mike thinks, and he thinks about her a lot.

He and his wife. They've never had children. Why not treat Consuela as their own, put her through college? The least he can do (he congratulates himself on being such a good Samaritan) given all the captain has done: chumming the rock and rooster fish, the cabrilla and tuna for the big spenders, the big talkers, sporting their head-to-toe saltwater camo. "Poncho. *Esta noche*, we have a fiesta," Mike Spanglishes, the purple palm trees on his shirt stuck to his perspiring skin. "Celebrate the education of Consuela." He slaps Poncho on the back. "Bring your *familia*."

On his way home, Poncho fishes off the shore. Nylon string weighted with rusty washers and wrapped around a piece of driftwood. Swings the line like a lariat. He sees the snapper, ghost-like, inside the pale silk of the lifting wave. His beached, waiting panga leans to one side, its bright turquoise hull like cool thought, like absence, like leaving. Standing on the bow, a pelican dries its feathers, its wings outstretched, as though crucified, as though victorious.

In that moment it becomes clear to Poncho. Without their dollars he can still fish; without him, their dollars and Sims waders can't hook *nada*. The realization feels like something akin to happiness or power.

Elena and Consuela wash their faces using water saved in the enameled basin. Poncho combs palmate through his hair until it shines like a black limousine. His wife coils her long braids tight. Consuela puts on her glowing white *quincenera* dress from last year. They walk to the hotel.

Popping the bottle cap with his teeth, Mike shakes a naked Barbie in Poncho's face. "Got to *finito* the lures. We got work to do, *hombre*, before hurricane season, *tormentas*. In one month, fishing over." He sticks out his chin, punches it with his fist to illustrate how the tip of the Baja juts out into the ocean. "This mangy peninsula just asks to be hit. Time to get out. And that's what this party's about. In a month. Consuela to San Diego. A room all her own. Good education. She'll visit you and Elena on her *vacaciones*. *¡Opportunidad! ¡Futuro! ¡Futura!* Whatever."

Poncho watches Mike wipe beer from his mouth. Lacking the English answer, Elena puts her hand to her lips. Poncho looks to his daughter.

"We got all dressed up, *Señor* Mike," says Consuela. "Such a pleasure. *Gracias* for dinner."

"You surely did," he says looking her over.

"All dressed up," says Consuela, "to say no."

Run, Run

Run, run. The boys run from their one room shanty. Two beds
for four. Cardboard boxes as makeshift shelves. They run, run
past rice and beans simmering on the stove, the refrigerator
that shivers and sweats, past school uniforms spread-eagled
to dry on the red bougainvillea. Their school teaches about
evolution and prime numbers. Their mother and father—
about Jesus, miracles, and Armageddon. The boys run
to smell U.S.A. on her skin. Run, run.

Curlicued

I made a promise to myself I wasn't going
to think about your chisels, bull nose rabbet
plane, the whorls of cedar on the shop floor
curlicuing our initials every time. But I broke it.

Had we never known what it was to be bowlined
within each other's salty embrace this would not
be a sad poem. It would be a happy one about
dreaming boats, your even strokes of less

then more across our naked current, beaching
on the islands of my wrists, our scalloped sleep.
This would be about setting sail to each other, filling
spinnakers of years-from-now with dazzle—

dazzle it turns out we didn't dare so had no business
believing. Maybe if I'd learned to loft a lap strake
hull to fit the palm of your embrace, diagram
a thwart spanning boatwright to me, draft perfectly

the exquisite fullness of your being, then this would be
a poem about sailing, together, in December, from Costa Rica
to the Caribbean.

Bigger Idea

That night I step out
the distance between
the wall and the door
to calculate the space
needed for
a bigger idea.

In front of my rented
cabina, I pick up iguana
shit, feel the warmth of it
through the plastic bag
against my palm.

Parque de Reptilandia

A turtle tied to a string swims away.
Young boys reel it back in. It tries
again. This turtle can't win. The zookeeper
walks past with a bucket of squirming
white rats. Cage opened. One with tiny toes
and pink ears is thrown in. Whiskers twitch.
It inches along the branch toward the motion-
less constrictor. Inquisitive. Trusting. Closer.
Closer. They touch noses. It looks like
a kiss. I want to believe it's a kiss.

Big Island Triptych

I PIDGIN
Too many broke da mout big bumbucha meals.
Now her opu bumbucha too. She fat. Sun has slow-
cooked this white opake-woman. She wrinkled.
Look moke like leather. Hang down breasts
slow hula under muumuu. She hopin' gray
haired mainland brah with vacation home
da one she been waiting on. Thought of him
gives her chicken skin. Scooters his way,
coconut oil in her satchel to make her slick.
Green and blue balloons hangin' on neighbor gate.
Someone else's wedding or anniversary happen. She late.

II FROG
Wal Mart's the culprit. More precisely, a shipment
of flowers from Orlando to the new Hilo store. Stowaway:
the quarter-sized coqui. At first it seemed like fun.
Employees chanting: Find the froggie! Now, they're
10,000 per acre. After sundown, you can't hear yourself
think. Ninety decibel peeps. No snake or tarantula to even
the score. Frogs feast on insects the native plants require.
Retirees-turned-*vigilantes* patrol in golf carts at dusk, nuke
any they find with acid spritzer. Nothing bad ever happened
here before, unless you count brutal beheadings by early-day
kahunas or now, dead coral reefs and skipjack die-offs...that sort of thing.

III ALPHABET
Everything hulas and sways here, has soft,
come-hither hips: the grasses, the breezes, fish
in the black pumice corrals, anemones fingering
the floor of the sea. And the language. All words,
every syllable must end with a vowel; all consonants
(only seven) be followed by a, e, i, o or u; and no two
consonants can cohabit, ever. The result? Not enough
consonant power to put up a fight, to get spitting
mad. The only one who tells it like it is,
is Pele. But even her spittle and hair form fine
lava lace that floats serenely on the ocean
after her mightiest eruptions, her obsidian
tears like jewels encased in white heat. No
wonder the missionaries, kahunas, coquis
and haoles have had their way. Consonants wanted.

Impressions

See the man swing and throw his net.
The woman holding a purple parasol walking
the red clay road.

The unblinking eyeball of the fried tilapia.
Mariana's handmade doll, crab claw hands
resting on limpet hips.

Chicken wings sizzling on burning fronds.
The hairy, brown coconut cut open—the liquid inside
like first milk, watery, thin.

See the girl's crutches make round impressions
in the dirt. The store-bought breasts of the missionary's
wife immobile under her dress.

The starving dogs. The sloth not moving. The rubbery,
cone-shaped flower in Felipe's garden that releases
perfumed tears when touched.

Your troubles are but pumice— they will float in my love. See
the wake of your kicking, a calligraphy of foam. See the cave leading
to the ocean fill and empty with the waves, like a mouth
opening and closing, gasping for air.

Fisherman's Beach: A Requiem

Isidro launches his panga from Fisherman's Beach,
the only sheltered cove on the coast. Streaks a white
wake across the bay like sky-writer on blue below.
Hand on throttle, he points the bow. Big-hipped
swells roll rhythmic under his aluminum arrow.
He scans for worry lines on the glassy surface,
telling of fish chased by something much
bigger; spies scales of brume brick-bracking
overhead. Every fisherman knows the signs:
"Mackerel sky, not 24 hours dry."

Must hurry. *Prisa*. Cast, cast again. Hours pass.
Clouds build.Captains spur sluggish hulls heavy
with catch through hammering white-capped chop.
Taking on water. Cove in sight. Catch swell,
miss, u-turn, again, full speed, gun it, lift motor!
Isidro surfs panga to perfect slide-stop on beach,
like his father, uncle, grand and great...exactly here,
exactly this way for many thousands of days.

Salt-licked *capitans* clean their catch. Buyers from La Paz,
Todos Santos match bids. Frenzied pelicans and gulls
squabble for guts, heads. All this by the grotto near
the lagoon, the shrine for Our Lady of the Big
Ocean, Our Lady of the Big Catch, Our Lady
of Everything but the one they forgot: Our Lady
the Protector of Fisherman's Beach. American
developer in big cowboy hat practices laughing
in Spanish. The fishermen don't get the joke,
agree he needs more practice. "*Soprecita*," he repeats,
laughing again. "A little surprise..." and, under his breath:
"guaranteed to capsize the life you've known." Gestures
to stakes in the sand flying plastic streamers. "Not
Fisherman's' Beach anymore. It's mine."

II

Scale House

Scale House

On the other side of this desert,
these mountains, there's still more
West. (I stopped, after travelling
2,700 miles in that direction, to avoid
the possibility of meeting up with myself,
settled for somewhere shy of my imagined
Eden.) Here, sage leans its small grey shoulders
into the scorch of day. Desert lilies push through
pebbles of pumice. This notion of blooming
in volcanic ash, I have come to understand.

How dreamlike now, those years with him,
the days I'd haze our cows, culls and dries,
onto the platform scale. My husband (he died
in '08 – "dead as a nit" is how the hired man
put it) would joggle the weights into the notches,
write the totals on paper scraps, fragments
of my discarded poems.

Black Baldy # 275, 1500 pounds
scrawled on the back of "lives
are designed to fly"; *Hereford # 313,
1700 pounds* on the reverse of "I know
there's love somewhere in all of this"
the balance arm floating in carefully
calibrated space. The whole time
our stock dog would sit, wagging, staring
at one spot on the scale house wall. He heard
something (a mouse?) behind the boards.
He'd wait it out. However long it took.

Behind this desert, these mountains I hear
a sound (a promise?). Something. I'm waiting
it out. "Next!" my husband would bark, all business.
Playful then, I'd take a turn, step on the scale
and watch as he calculated the weight of my life
as countered by hope.

Red Flag

Love-struck, she agrees to cross the ocean of sagebrush
tucked under the aging Irishman's arm, a hummingbird
snug beneath the wing of a migrating snow goose.

He wears a moth-eaten stocking cap, boots as long as her thigh,
an old down parka that bleeds feathers from barbed wire tears,
calls "Hey girls" to his broody cows as he pitchforks hay.

She loves him for all that and for his uneven bars of spontaneous
jitterbug, mad genius and song, for smelling like wood smoke,
pheromone of passion to the smitten stowaway.

But soon this pale Irish molts inconstancy and white heat, lusts
for her but even more for the taste of his own blood, comes
charging out of imagined corners all spittle and fight.

Later, contrite, he pens "Love you" adding the lazy-eight of infinity
to ease the pain of a broken promise neither one made, only surmised,
based on the alignment of their—what—stars? Goose down? Right.

He places a note in the mailbox, red metal flag raised to signal the postman.
Out of nowhere a hummingbird, fooled by the rouge, the flare, tries to drink
imagined nectar from the flag-not-flower, the honey-less object of its desire.

Him and Carl

Ramrodding down the dirt road,
sage flat.
Blue heeler leans into the breeze,
ears flap.
Calves scamper through the rabbit brush,
tails crook'd.
Dust boils behind the pickup,
rattle trap.
Airborne over the cattle guard
on the rise
that separates Carl's place from his.

God damn.
Spots another truck.
Starts to slow.
Gears down just right
so what
was stirred up behind
won't overtake.

They pull up alongside,
shift their chew.
"Whatcha doing, Carl?
"Going down the road."
Both nod, because it's true.

A man can leave at any speed.
It's the coming together that takes finesse.
They both know about this.

Untitled

Day floods the prairie
Lone rider goes at a lope
The fence line is down

Rose, a Retrospective

Her color inspired the name, Country
Squire emblazoned on her flank. Later the s-q-u
would fall off. Country ire. My sentiments exactly,
considering the hours I spent behind her wheel
transporting tractor parts and groceries.

I would set up a playpen in the back. My children
rolled like marbles when I made the turn from dirt
to pavement to head for town. "You again?" the state
trooper would ask as I gunned it home before the ice
cream melted, before sundown.

Dog drool smudged Rose's windows, from noses
eager for airborne news. Under her hood there were
strands of straw, traces of the field mice who moved
in. Their blind babies, when aroused by the heat
and motion, crawled out across my feet. And between
the seats, chewed bits of Zwieback that escaped small
hands on the way back from a branding or delivering
lunch to the crew.

She rode the ruts like a cruise ship, absorbing the worst
of everything. Rocks thrown by the grader, hapless birds
into her grill. One pitch black night, horses in the road
rolled, hooves up, flailing, eyes white and over the hood of Rose.

Together she and I carried my firstborn home. Years
later we watched my husband grow small
in the rearview mirror. One dog and three
children along for the ride of our lives.

A young family bought her just as mine were looking
for cars of their own, had long since stopped kissing
Rose on her snout to thank her for safe journeys.
She was showing her age, stalling out at intersections.
I embraced her away from the view of the buyers,
lovingly ran my hand along the back of her seats,
the smooth sheen of her fender, across the nicks and dents
we had endured together. I lay down across her hood.
She sagged affectionately beneath me.

I'd see her around from time to time and would introduce
myself, over again, to the new owner. "We're fixing to
fill her up even more!" the young woman said, patting
her pregnant stomach. And she and Rose would amble
off, listing this way and that, all shocks and absorbers gone.

The last time was this time last fall. Looking for a used truck
for my son. The place had once been someone's home. The farm
house now a sales room. The former garden forgotten. Fruit trees
riddled with dead limbs. Parked in the yard were used cars, pick-ups.
Some merited the false cheer of balloons attached to a wiper or a brightly
colored decal proclaiming a special deal. There in the back was Rose,
her torn seats oozing sponge-rubber, her grill punctured, her side
trim stripped, her blushing countenance now muted, tires flat,
energy spent. "Rose, Rose," I whispered into her vent.

Consultation Over a Chew

there's his map
in the back pocket of his dungarees
telling them
a moment ago
that Isabelle to Otterdam
was too far to drive
for the next rodeo

"keep your finger on Isabelle, beau..."

a tobacco spit
straight and even
shaped by two front teeth
must be a quarter inch between 'em

"Otterdam", he finally said
"way the hell over here beyond Terry
can't do 'er, beau
another time instead, mebbe"

so he folded up the map
careful and slow
along careworn creases
as though
a gas station map
was something to treasure

and down off the fence they got
silent
not a jump
but like snakes off a rock

Chicken Slaughter

The clothes hanger bent to a hook, I sneak up
on the hen grubbing in the yard, snag her
by one leg. Upside down, she surrenders, wings
flung overhead like a Sussex Sabine, her small brain
topsied, hunt and peck turvied, her sky suddenly
underfoot. I right-side her, smooth her feathers,
tuck her under my arm, slowly stroke her beak
between lizard-lidded eyes until she's spellbound.
Then flop her thin neck across the stump and, with
the kitchen hatchet, chop off her decorated pate.

It's true about running around like a chicken
with its head cut off, lifeblood spilling over the bare
ground, involuntarily carrying on, without thought, plan,
or direction—but looking for all the world like a living
thing playing itself out. I kick the dogs away, grab the witless
squab, dunk her in the steaming pot that looses the hold
of her dimpled skin, then spank her like a newborn. Thickets
of soggy down fall around my feet, scuttle across the dirt.
Naked as the day is new, she is ready to be gutted: tiny insides
removed, tiny heart and remains of cricket and corn, gizzards
and cluck box—when pressed offering one last word.

Soon the hen I'd fed and tendered is on the counter,
pink and clean, little drumstick arms extended, weighing in
the same as the neighbor's preemie. My children like to play
with the severed, rubbery legs, pull the tendons, watch the trident
toes curl; they learn a thing or two about contraction, putting food
on the table, voluntary and involuntary reaction.

Afternoon Light

He presses down
the top strand
so she can clear
the barbed wire,
gives her his hand,
hopes
her up and over.

He opens
the gate, waves
her through,
latches it tight
so the before
won't come
after.

Taking the wheel,
he climbs
the ridge,
takes the roadless
to a view
she'd forgotten
mattered.

He stops short there.
The redwings shush
to hear what
mister long
and tall will
tell her.

*The sun's still
high in the sky,*
he says. *Least ways,
high enough
for this feller.*

Rancher Gets Metaphysical

sometimes snow does share sky's space
you can take three steps between flakes
you don't think just snow or just sky

i wonder about snow
daring to move in on sky's place
setting out stakes

Fall Desert Blooms Yellow

Leslie Gulch

Monstrous jagged compound fractures, undressed
wounds, bleeding titans, ghouls and gargoyles,

their thousand rock mouths scoured round
by wind and water. They whistle "oooh" in unison,

as time passes across welded tuff lips, "oooh" to behold at their feet
the display of impermanent hue, desert blonde and dizzy,

rabbit brush's fall flavesence, canary song, lemon chiffoning trailside.
How gay, these frilly Rockettes, in the morning mist.

A desert ruche of jonquil and cream, midday hawking their sere
brightness to lure sluggish bees weighing the value of daytime efforts

against recent cold. And with the scrim of evening—chroma jazz, a riff of
   dark
goldenrod in the gloaming. Soon this flaxen celebration will end, the telling
   pallor,

confirming this season's blooms are past pollination.

Desert Keep

Dedicated to the High Desert Museum, Bend, Oregon

Silent moon the desert keeps.
Coyote keens who yip yip who
to gargling raven, drover, lynx,
parrot-nosed mustang, leather chinks,
to Paiute drumming up the sun,
cradle board and beaded dreams,
to cleated rigger, swabber, saw,
in forests thick with Ponderosa.

Coyote keens who yip yip who
beware, beware or soon, too soon
here only here you'll pan for fools,
bronco bust, ride coarse split rail,
finger vials from Kam Wah Chung,
roll your knuckles in the swail
of salt licked by dumber tongues.

Coyote sings take care, take care
or soon it's only here you'll come
to practice stunted distance vision,
peer at dioramas that pretend
forests, sage steppes gone, forgotten.

Coyote warns beware, beware.
Don't let the asphalt world overtake
you who slept with birthing mare,
head resting on her heaving flank,
measured your gaze against crazed bull,
chased giddy pig corner to corner,
netted salmon from the exuberant falls,
felled your child's future in the tall tree woods,
laid down windrows of sweet alfalfa.
Coyote sings who yip yip who.

Nowhere Called Home

we drive the long way
past sagebrush and juniper
veer off Route Twenty

horses hightail it
prairie dogs fold tiny hands
cows raise up their heads

the valley narrows
we shadow the riverbed
to nowhere called home

Night Hawk

Daylight. Riveted

    by my commitment to

        night, I stop flying to roost on thunder

eggs that mimic my lichen-like

    hues streaked

        with white, because

darkness is what I need to grease

        these wings, to dive down sheer

    canyon walls, hijacking mosquitoes

      in flight, to ascend again,

  trailing a filament of whistle.

Another Round

chugging beer
to some country western
at a whistle stop
like them in Billings
the band in chords of blue
and silver threads on their backs
sings songs of trains and Tulsa
and Miles City memories
oh and Irv
he's quite the rounder
asks the waitress if
when she has some time
to spare
she might
you know
where
a laugh's a slap
on the side
of a leg up
to a life
that's good
not one
of wishes
penciled
in the margins

Loudest Sounds

Sugar cookies cool on last week's community
section, leaving a buttery stain on outdated
stories—hardware store shuts down, another farm
auction, town's only physician retiring. Near
as she can tell, only thing working is the wind,
loosening shingles and window panes, lifting nails,
chasing litter down alleyways.

Time was she'd tie poems to willows along the old
rail bed where folks walked at dusk, coyotes
calling. Before the grocery closed, before fuel
and feed costs got so high, before hope dried up...
used to be lots more folks out walking. She'd slip
the verse into small ziplocs, secure them to the branches
with a wire tie.

She slides her shopping list from under the belly
of the pumpkin sitting on her counter. She's fixing
to make pie. Tomorrow she'll go to get what
she needs—all the way to Boise. The lids on the glass jars
of peaches pop, signaling a seal. She taps each one
to make sure. Loudest sounds all day. She feels like
the last one here.

She leans down, lifts off the floor a giant tumbleweed
festooned with poems, tosses it out the door.

Fly Already

The covey's tri-toes tickle-tap
forth and back across wooden
planks, tiniest staccato riff
on accidental xylophone –
a sun-warmed boardwalk
between cabin and stock pond.
At first languor, then lightning
as beeps, warning of imagined
predator, spread like downy fire
through the alarmed octet. Faster,
faster footwork—the first line
of frantic response, as though
the wings they sport are only
for effect or, at best, the plan
of last resort. Fly, fly already
because you can.

Mothering-up

Bag swollen to bursting, the brindle cow wallered for her calf, the one my father had gathered up hours before—bloody, lifeless, off the barn floor. "Give a hand, son." I was ten. My mother dead as many years by then. Father strung the dead calf by its feet from a beam, skinned its silky hide clean.

My old Blue Heeler Lucy turns up bloated in the river where it goes through town. I'm real choked up. She's been my best friend since I was twenty-one, year I left the farm. I fish her out. I set her in the front seat of my truck. We take a day to visit our favorite spots.

My father used a crow bar to split the pelvis of the slim-hipped, baldy heifer. She buckled in pain, choked to death in the stanchion. But he saved her calf, rubbed the shivering thing dry with hay, then holding it up, a kind of crazed look in his eye, he wrapped the brindle calf's steaming hide around the orphan's back, tied it with twine run through holes he made with an ice pick in the skin.

"Lucy, here's where you'd swim for a stick." Lucy's gaze is fixed. I'm crying again. Our final stop before rigor mortis sets in: the rendering plant outside of town. The man looks at me and Lucy strange-like. "This takes the fuckin' cake," he says. "Sure, grafting an orphaned calf, but a mutt? And a rank one at that. You must be nuts."

My father ran the frantic, big-bagged brindle into the pen. Pretty quick she was fooled, nuzzled and licked her dead calf's cloak, let the imposter bull calf suck, took him as her own. Watching I wondered, had I ever been any mother's son?

The man hangs Lucy from a hook, cuts razor-clean slices above her paws, behind her ears, under her tail and chin, peels off her coat like he's done it every day since time began. Before pulling out on the road, I take Lucy's hide, drape it over my back, tie it tight across my chest with twine run through holes I make with an ice pick in her skin.

Skin-Walker

The grange is full. Ranchers come to wrangle
about wolves. Seaton Tuttle goes first: "Up
on Crow Creek had to shoot my bull after a pack
took him down. Ate out his liver. The bastard still
breathin' when I found him. Call you Fish and Game
folks right away to register the kill so as to get
my government rebate check. Fair enough deal. But
you jokers take your sweet Uncle-Sam-issued-green-
pick-up-time. By then some hard rain tap tapped
the tracks away." He mimics the raindrops with his fingers,
balletic, cynical. "In the end you sorry sons of bitches
claimed it was a cow dog killed my prize Angus. Just to keep
my money in your wallets is my guess. No cow dog ever
do such in the Wallowas or Blues. I'm here to tell you,
it was wolves."

Seaton sounds tough alright. Fact is he doesn't dare look
the government man in the eye. He heard tell wolves
cause blindness. He's thinkin' maybe people soft on them
do too. If he ever nabs a wolf...or a softy...he swears
he'll hang its counterfeit hide on his barbed wire fence,
ward off any others with bright ideas. Likely these wives
tales is nonsense, but then...a person never really knows
for sure. As far as Seaton is concerned, this honyaker
Federali is half beast, has a pact with Satan to cross-fence
all his dreams with rules and fees.

"Our studies show," says the ranger, "wolves force
elk herds to split, move them off creeks and streams."
He points at a map with a stick. "Here willows—
delicate, leafy green— coming back. Fish habitat—deep,
cold pools—same thing. Slap of beavers heard again."
Ranchers shift in their chairs. Grumble some. He goes on.
"Wolves leave carcass, carrion for lynx, beetles, ravens.
It's wolves, wolves, I'm telling you, make us whole again."

Seaton takes a second look, swears he sees a furry
ear sticking out from under the fast talker's cap.
Something's rank about the whole deal. Doesn't smell
right. Meeting adjourns, the ranchers gun their trucks
into the Wallowa night, spitting gravel out from under
their tires, curses out their pick-up windows. They aren't
buying this holy reincarnated dog. It stands for all
that is wrong in their lives: taxes, bored wives,
teasel in the fields, high fuel prices.

Next meeting a week later. Government man waits.
Nobody shows. *When ranchers go silent only means
one thing,* he thinks. *Taken matters into their own hands.*
He races out of the room, drives fast toward the vanishing
sun, to the canyon that cradles the Imnaha and Snake.
Gets out of his rig, checks for tracks, listens for sounds,
and, seeing no one's around, like quicksilver, shape-shifts
from man to *lobo.* His furry head cocked back, black nose
to the heavens, he keens low to high to warn his wolf brethren.

Now, on moonless summer nights in the Wallowas
and Blues, after the Calliope hummingbirds nurse
the red streaks from the sunset, when owls call
for a mate, and crickets fall silent to wait out the dark,
on these nights the only light is a spot, the only sounds
the howl of the wolf and the click of rifles off safety.

Palindrome

"Madam, never odd or even" or how about "Nurses
run." Parlor game brain teasers. Entertaining until
they're not, until genetic codes are scrambled
by the covert repeat, the lethal patterned repetition
colonizing the unsuspecting allele. Unable to resist,
the helix unravels...a slow, unspiraling death.

In a year,
just one,
my friend lost daughter and son
to this stealth dystrophy.

I distract my grief by railing against a no-show
God. It doesn't help. What does is going
for a walk with you. I clamber up the junipered
slope, praise the desert's beauty, find solace
in the natural order. Until you point out
the ground's overrun with Medusahead,
deceptively pretty in its refrain of carefully
crafted coronas, latticed back-to-front sameness,
as it strangles life out of this basin and range.

In a year,
just one,
the winter feed ground
is under siege
by these noxious weeds.

We return to the log house at dusk, witness
the intersection of sun set, moon rise, the promise
implicit in the meeting of two different
manifestations of braided light. We're thankful
to have finally stopped repeating our mistakes forward
and backward, backward and forward, or we'd never
have survived to behold this moment.

In a year,
just one,
we come undone.

Full Attention

November 9, 2016

Morning after rout. Shut out din – pollsters,
hucksters. Get in truck, shove sandwich,
MoonPie into glove box, thermos under seat,
load up the dogs, turn the key, step on the gas,
head for McKay Creek.

Look there...black cattle, moony in morning sun,
dotting yellow stubble; thick trunks of Ponderosa
flanking roadway stutter light-then-dark.
Switch back coming up. Lower gear. Shimmy
over cattle guard. Change jumps in cup holder.
Rough going from here.

Bolted gate. Pull up. What the hell. Metal
buckled near in two. Some angry, counterfeit
SOB forcing entry. Jockey combination
Drive through. Lock up. Careful now. Sheer
drop into Mitchell canyon. Ever find
the precipice inviting? Final hardpan mile
to the summit of Stephenson Mountain.

Lower tailgate. Set dogs loose. Open
cabin same as if November 7: unlock
shutters and door, set out wash basin,
fill the kerosene lantern, clean the grate,
start a fire, snuff match between forefinger
and thumb, listen for pack rats in the ceiling.
Small things, do small things with full
attention.

And when evening halos the hills, walk
shoeless on golden carpet of tamarack
needles. Push boughs of white fir aside.
Dodge their quick return. At the ridge,
sit on favorite rock. Look out. Look out.

Pack up, leave at dawn, mug of coffee in hand.
The sun won't have returned to the valley yet.
Be some time before it does.

III

Jamestown Bridge

Jamestown Bridge

From a distance, the bridge
spears the sky, bares bolted canine
teeth of braided steel, its lofty girded
spires obscured by a dark cloud.
I cry out loud to my father, silent
at the wheel, to my mother silent
next to him: "Stop! Turn around!"

Don't they understand our car will flip,
slide down the sheer, slatted face
of the four-lane cliff into the churning
chop? The drowned end of our small
effort at family sealed inside
our two-door? We have no business
on such a steep incline to the other
side of things.

My protests puncture their silence. They speak
of the bridge, the far shore, bemoan this child
should have such fears. "We've come this far,"
my father sighs, pays the toll, down shifts.
My mother reaches over the seat, puts
a hand on my knee. "It is never quite as bad
as you think. You'll see."

Entering the Boys' School Dining Hall

Every Sunday the throng of hungry boys
would part like a corduroy and gabardine
sea to let her mother and schoolmaster father
through,

then crowd in for, if lucky, a stealth feel
of the winsome faculty daughter's emerging
breasts she herself had scarcely noticed.

She realizes now that for all those boys-to-men, in their
requisite striped school ties knotted tight at the chin,
she was the innocent object of their clumsy dreams.

Surely for a twelve-year-old girl this lust fest, this public
undressing, couldn't have been a good thing.

Townie

Her flock, and others like them,
arrive the same time each July,
fling open their musty summer houses
to the breezes off Buzzards Bay,
feather the reclaimed seasonal nests
with summer slipcovers yanked
over the wingback and the chaise
with the same vigor the maid uses
to pull the undershirt over Isabelle's
blonde head each brackish morning.

After a poached egg with toast
Isabelle is tutored in what it is
to be summer people. About old
money versus nouveau, never
to go bare-armed in public, or
heaven forbid, associate with townies,
who live in the same place,
twelve months of the year.

Forget that — she thinks Anthony Olivera
is fine. She'd heard he kissed a girl
one time. He always wears a sleeveless
undershirt. His skin is dark, muscled,
slick. His hair black, luscious, thick.
He helps in his father's grocery store.
Can reach behind and, without looking,
grab sodas off the shelf: Nehi, Coke,
Root Beer. He knows just where
they are; can close the cash register
drawer with his hip, make change without
moving his lips.

Anthony has a water ski boat. It is blue,
black and silver, is called Rip Tide.
Isabella has a sailing dinghy, all white save
a thin green line along the hull. She heads
it into the wind. Sails luffing, she leans
out over the stern and, taking pains,
with bright red paint gives her boat
a new name.

Snack Mix

You'd think the snack packet passed out
on the plane—twists, sticks, nuggets—
(pretzel, cheddar, corn) would have held
more crunchy bites of that consonant blend
but there were only 15 (I counted) mini whatsits
in the blue air-sealed baglet. Astonishing,
Herculean even, that those tiny few could contain
55 so-called ingredients within their diminutive
crispy contortions, require 500 pharma non-
words to describe them. Ten, at most, bona fide
food, the rest—rogue gangs of -oses,
-ates and –iums marching under the flag
of the unstated but implied: carcinogen.

I'm not stupid. No pawn of mega-corps. I read
the small print: fructose, folic, phosphate, mono-
hydrate. I'm on to the Nestles and Frito-Lays
who want to keep me at multi-syllabic bay about
what I'm ingesting: artificial everything, built-in
cravings, accelerated endings. But this one?
"Silicon dioxide"? It's glass!

Did everyone else know this? Hey, sideshow
freaks, we're swallowing shards of glass crushed
into granules, added to anything not supposed
to cake. Bet I've eaten enough in my breakfasts
that an ornate, silicate chandelier has reconstituted
in my gut, lighting up the rosy, moist grottos,
the gathering bubbles of indigestion, the sloughing signs
of exhaustion, defeat and physical disintegration;
a candelabrum, intricate, with tiny suspended crystal
tear drops that weep for me, for us all, witless, complicit.

Stare Down

Moss coats bison-sized thunder
trunks of wind and fire-fall, former
Goliaths now back-ridden across thrash
of rocks and raucous river castanet-ing
ouzel and trout in tumble time with autumn's end.

Despite the late seasonal hour, despite
the cold, despite the garden of brawling
otter-slick river stones and crestfallen logs,
there—a white collared aster brightly trained
on what happens by. "It can't be real," the hiker
posits. "Maybe it's plastic, a riverside shrine
to a reckless teen fish taking the river twists too fast."

If the shrine shtick was funny, you wouldn't
know it from the daisy. It returns the human's
gaze, unblinking, inscrutable. "It *is* real!" the hiker
exclaims, getting closer. "So out of place, time,
season." He should talk.

Closer

She has a way about his kitchen.
Her hand on his counter, his sponge—
slow, more a caress. *Her* faucet,

her cutting board. She impales squares
of cantaloupe, halved purple grapes,
skewers them in the upside down dome

of the season's first watermelon. Shish-
kebobs for hair, oranges for eyes, pineapple
nose, strawberry mouth—a startled alien,

fruity voodoo, staring as I, the new girl-
friend, surrender my ready-made store-
bought I've brought in my hot car. She

insists: "Let me help you. You look so
tired." She places my Sara Lee next
to her rhubarb made from scratch. I can't

make out the tined pattern in her perfect crust.
A heart? To let off steam. How does she know
the extra roll of paper towels is stored

at the very back of the cupboard to the right
of the sink? She insists on a photo of me
and my new friend. "Closer together, you

love birds." With a familiar ease she downloads
the shot onto his computer with the caption:
potluck. Her trailing smile confirms

what I first guessed, now know. She has leaned
up against the counter between his fridge
and oven more than a time or two.

Birthday Bouquet

At my door—a bouquet, the instructions for care
held in the tines of a plastic trident inserted
between twists of holly, goatees of pine.

        Fresh Fun!
        (I'm down!)
        Fill Me Up!
        (I've begged as much in moments of passion.)
        Be Cool!
        (Directed to me? Play hard to get? Is that
        what that landed these velvet-wristed blossoms?)
        Preserve and Protect. Trim stems
        (Regrets? Expectations?) **using a sharp**
        knife. *(Be bold, decisive?)* **Add**
        preservative as needed. *(But you said*
        you find me beautiful.) **If roses wilt** *(Exhaustion, neglect –*
        I know all about it.) **submerge**
        in a bowl of warm water and straighten.
        (Analysis? Not again.) **Cut two inches off**
        the stem under water *(The type of torture*
        therapists love.) **and leave there**
        two hours. *(See what I mean? That's a long*
        time for a flower. Not death but near.)
        Don't Chew Me Up! Don't Swallow
        Me! *(...whole. If you did, I'd have to*
        leave.)
        Watch, Grow, Enjoy!
        (If you say so. How hard can that be?
        Very.)

Mud Puddle Tavern

Dedicated to Robert Michael Pyle, Lepidopterist, Author and Poet

American Copper sidles up to the bar at the Mud Puddle Tavern. Long, hot, high altitude day of display at Hells Canyon. He folds up on top of a dung chip, wings pulsing. *Gimme a urate, neat.* Butler's Alpine serves it straight. By the time the others show up, his proboscis is deep in his third Blue Bell. *Offered a Pearly Everlasting for a go at her bursa copulatrix,* he slurs. *And more.*

Red Admiral and Great Spangled Fritellary roll their compound eyes. *Whatever. You two randy butterflies, you get all the ladies,* says Checker. *So I'm a little rough around the forewing. Bird strikes. Thought women found that sexy. Why does she flash that photonic thing anyway, flaunt those sultry black spots on those gossamer orange wings? Some sexy headlights. I invited her to go end to end with me in the honey suite at the root of the corn lily. Said I'd caress her thorax every six-legged way, trace the curves of her spiracles with my tongue, fill that empty cavity with everything in me for when her eggs go sashaying by. Not enough. Not even my cache of urate as nuptial gift. That ruddy lady closed her wings to me. When she did, she vanished. Blended into the Indian Paintbrush. Well, she can just pheromone herself to the moon for all I care.*

All the rest who'd been denied on the high alpine reaches rub their forelegs together in sympathy. Persius among them. *I'll get Checkerspot to give you a lift home,* he says. *You've got to watch out for these trickster ladies, man. Now you see them, now you don't. Could be a bad luck faerie. Or worse. Goddess. Turn you into something objectionable.*

The Philatelist and Penny Black

He'd waited a long time for a shot
at a Penny Black. What's one more
year, day, a few hours among
practitioners of the king's hobby,
the ultimate collectible at hand?

Between business trips he waited
straight-backed on her davenport. Might
as well be dead, she thought, walking
in. But her sudden appearance filled
his balloon-art body with artificial glee.
He wagged his blown-up head, tossed
his arms, jigged his distended knees
and promised her, if she'd just say yes,

the deal of the century: a used traveling
man, four million miles of sadness,
some neglect. And get this. Delta Air
gave him a prize for spending his life
in their skies. He got to decide: a pearl
necklace or rolling suitcase. He chose
the pearls, for Penny, but she was running
late. No problem. He could wait.

That's what scares her about him. This
ability to slow his pulse during times
of cold, as though he knows, and she
doesn't, that he has already wet
her gummed adhesive, a little, enough,
to seal an eventual fate. All he has
to do is wait.

He puts the pearls by a fire he won't
light until he tweezes Penny Black again,
slips her into the waiting parchment sleeve,
completing the set. Meantime he air-
mails himself to another thousand
meetings in hotel boxes filled with
miniature ideas, soaps and shampoos;
and after, departing Concourse A, B
or eternity, returns to his absent house
and the pursuit of his lonely hobby.

If only, she'd thought when she
visited, the curtains weren't so shut,
the present so forgotten. On a table
littered with stamps, she gazed at one
with infinitesimal cattle grazing.
"1892 Columbian. Worth gold, but not
as dear as my Penny Black," he'd said
pulling her to him. She lifted the magnifier
to examine more closely the hallmark
of his heart, for the first time spying
the tiny puncture left by another lover
heedless of the great value of such things.
But only when left undamaged.

Mr. Las Vegas

He eases into the cul-de-sac – buffed black roadster, dancing
silver hubs – offers her the passenger side, closing the door behind
her shimmering summer ankles. She places her manicured hand
on his cologned perfection and they go,

drive out of town, past garish billboards glistening with sequined
women pulsing neon: "Come back and see me again." He's searching
for an open stretch, smooth, a place of no dispute, a svelte Siri devoid
of extremes of emotion. See how the small, imperceptible depression
of his foot on the gas

disproportionately affects forward motion. That's what he likes—
to achieve high speeds with no change in expression. It would have been
one kind of ending if a deer had sprung out right then and they had flown
off the road in terror and confusion, wheels spinning, trying to gain traction.

But perhaps as tragic, they kept going until whatever propelled them
was unimaginatively spent on dry cleaning and plastic house plants. And what
happened after that such a grave disappointment it doesn't bear repeating.

Summer Psalm

Every June the altar guild of St. Philip's unheated wooden
chapel sweeps out winter's accumulated dankness and doubt, *
plumps the cushions of faith, repairs the frayed edges of common prayer.

Red doors are reopened to summer residents, a seasonal occurrence
as reliable as the silver herring's run up the Mattapoisett River *
to spawn another cycle of hope.

The chancel window and altar brass play with the Light the parishioners
seek. Confessions and petitions are pressed through the white point *
of the steeple, decorating heaven with human confections.

The service over, the churchgoers carelessly spill on to the street, stopping
traffic with their jubilant sense that everything's going to turn out fine *
despite the facts of their lives.

Ladies Room During Intermission at the Opera

The lady in line said every time the tenor sang the baby moved
in her stomach. I think to myself: *starting now there will be no
sadness ever again.* I imagine this baby's wings folded inside
the cocoon of this billowing mother who had traveled milkweed
to milkweed on tattooed wings until she landed and whoever
he was, found her and they mated and now here she is, waiting
in line to pee and in a few weeks she'll have a baby.

"Last one on the right is empty."
"Thanks."

While unwinding the toilet paper I thought: *I wish you would
inseminate me with one thing you know for sure, so I would.*
 I flush.

*When you left after dinner you said: "You are going to forget why
this is a good idea." How do you know and that people can only
see those who travel at the same pace?*
I tuck in my blouse.

Tell me your speed and location so I can adjust.
I smooth my skirt, unlock the stall.

The butterfly doesn't experience being abandoned.

The automatic faucet doesn't see I am here.

Trees and flowers don't grieve.

The automatic towel dispenser doesn't see me either.

I line my lips with Rose Garden Glossy, work on embracing
being invisible given the new and unimproved contours. Wait.
I'd better stretch, ease the numbness that has settled around
the joints of my sorrows. My therapist says I am more and more
unknown to myself, so I keep making appointments. Rapid eye
movement, past life regression, he says, free the imagination.
Something in me says "Save your money, go on a vacation."

They're calling an end to intermission.

Cat on the Window Seat

"Mom?" They're worried. Their frayed tether
to the world just put a box of Meow Mix
on the breakfast table instead of Krispies.
Doubt already dances along their thin limbs,
crackling their trust in the world.

She snaps together sandwiches tied with string
cheese, stuffs them in brown sacks, her children's
names scrawled on the back. Go, don't, remember,
hurry she shouts as though all three were one.

If she had stopped for a minute, she'd have
noticed the damp indent in the pillow
from muffled sobs, a shredded photo,
a knotted rope out the window.

Kids off, she to work. The house is silent save
for the parakeet in its cage on top of the fridge.
It doesn't sing, rather hooks its beak on the latch,
over and again tries to lift it from the inside, to escape
the dish of seeds, egg cup of water, swinging trapeze.

That evening she shouts homework, dinner, fold, clean,
as though all three were one. On the way to bed
they discover a pile of yellow and green feathers,
the parakeet's run for freedom intercepted by the cat
that sits on the window seat cleaning its paws.

Kitchen Axe

I grab the kitchen hatchet to split
kindling, prop quarter rounds
up on the ground and deftly
shear them into dry, pungent
strips, my breath in the cold night
like a steam engine cresting
a winter pass. I know

the axe head is loose on its wooden
handle. Each back-swing I imagine
the possible arc of disaster, iron blade
hurtling through house window or lodging
in my chin or head, but I'm used to living
with eventuality. Plus, lack of time, cold
house wanting, and I, deficient in common
sense, take my chances until

my daughter's boyfriend tsk, tsks,
takes the bobble-headed device
and dunks it head first, Halloween-
and-apple-less, in a saucepan of water.
Later he carries the sated cleaver
outside, tap, taps the handle end,
settling its heavy head once and for all
on its swollen wooden shoulder. Look,
he says. Won't even need a wedge.
A wedge, I say. I'd never have
thought of it.

But as these stories go, the wooden handle eventually
puckers and shrinks, the head comes loose again.
I'm back to taking my chances.

Spider in the Sink

From your eight-legged hairy hang-spider body language
it appears you've concluded the sum total
of your sheer experience is slickly insurmountable.
You're stymied by the slippery white
slopes of your cold, immutable, enameled history.
Your porcelain past defines your present, has you beat.

But don't resign yourself to a life of circling the drain
of regrets – all those missed opportunities for that fat fly.
Take a spider stand, arachnid man! At least try! Build a web!
Bark! Something! Soapy deposits on those alabaster slopes
might provide a toe hold. You never know. What if
this octo-multiplied shape eclipsing the horizon of the sink
thinks better of spitting toothpaste on your despair, is instead
inclined to find a piece of paper, an old jelly jar,
coax you into that transparent tram and deliver you
to a world of rainbows and free-range flies on the other side
of the screen door.

Aunt Joy to Dinner

You once sent me, all the way from London, one china plate with cherry-
colored trim and blooms of *prima auricula* in a terra cotta center. On the back
the Wedgewood stamp and the name: Sarah's Garden. Each year since
I have added dinner, soup, salad, serving and butter. And now, finally,
I have a setting fit for you. Please, be seated at the head and tell me again

what you once said about tidying the house last thing each night, mending
and making do, folding the spread at the foot of the bed, my father as a boy,
the knick-knacks on your shelves, wartime glory, all the stories. Tell me
of your unshakable faith in God, of favorite walks across your beloved
island sod with your eager, devoted dogs. Tell me

again before you go how is it you so cheerily went toe-to-toe
with life, stared down sadness, vigorously carried on no matter?
Oh, must you leave? Before you do...your garden. I remember every
walkway, bloom, and stone, every bird house and feeder and especially
the colorful border with *prima auricula* in the terra cotta center.

Undoing

I forget the snarled reason
for the whole undone discussion,
the whole dropped stitch conclusion.
At this point what can I do but pull
the yarn kinked from days as a knit
or purl, let it scribble and scrawl
across the floor, until I reach the spot
where a stitch was dropped, a beat
missed, a clue ignored. And start
there, unravel cabled memories: your
carpenter's caress of the hand-hewn
writing desk, initialed lockets, love notes
in flawless penmanship that disguised
the hole woven in years ago. It's not
at the very start, not a question of casting
every stitch back on, but somewhere
slightly further along. I'll re-begin there
with hope that's the diameter of thread,
feeling lucky to have that much.

IV

The Next to Last Question

Picto-Prayers

A boulder crouches like a Poor Will
in hiding. Where the head would draw
into feathery shoulders, some aboriginal
has etched a dancing four-legged creature
in the stone. On the would-be wing,
a snake-like form pierces a circle,
a crescent moon beside.

Earnest birders hiking with life lists
stop, gather handfuls of sage to toss
on this impromptu basalt altar, mutter
spontaneous supplications to these ancient
artists they believe knew more than they
ever will.

But who is to say these pictos
aren't just billboards? Good hunting
and fishing ahead! Wild onions!
Or maybe native graffiti inscribed
just after passion's consummation? Little
Fawn and Rides-the-Wind did it here,
a moon phase indicating date, pierced circle—
the hot-blooded action.

Whatever. For me I need to picture elders
gathering here to ponder accordioned rimrock,
waterfowl chuck-chucking in the cattail
marshes, cool-rising dawn – and then, inspired,
thoughtfully carving a picto-prayer. I need
to believe they knew what I doubt: that beauty
this generous will never give out.

One Sudden Afternoon

Crater Lake

What of this loch of shocking blue? Earth's navel? A monocular Mazama
with a basalt iris of columned stone? (That Ghost Ship, that igneous fan-
fare on the far shore—all that's left of the 400,000-year-old volcanic hydra.)
What of it, you ask, you with your daypack, sunblock and camera, here
in your RV?

I'll tell you. Millennia of stuttered explosions braided hot-wired coils,
pulled extravagant taffy castles, rolled towering turrets from running strikes
of molten tambour slapped against andesite hips. Then, in a fit, Mazama
pitched the whole 13 cubic miles of her perfect, tangled beauty.

In one sudden afternoon central Oregon's garden of Eden—cypress,
sassafras, elephant— buried under scalding syrup. In the mountain's
imploded place a sapphire seductress came to nest in the panting caldera.
Blame Llao, blame the Makalak chief's beautiful daughter, blame Skell,
blame the oozing rhyodacites that sealed Mazama's rifts, gagging
the shouts of the fractious magma chambers.

Wise Natives avert their eyes, refuse what this liquid Cyclops dares:
look 2,000 feet into her gaze. You'll weep to see mother, lover, devil;
fall into the well of the unblinking mystery; be drawn to the unstable edge
of everything you thought you knew as you apprehend the scalding
deep-water plumes, seething fumaroles, vomiting lake-bottom bulges—
the guarantee a catastrophe is fire-branded to happen again. Maybe now.
Maybe to you.

Summer Lake in Spring

This fleeting lake's a shimmering silver platter. A kaleidoscope
of changing patterns, flight and color: flourishes of blue, green,
slate, then suddenly brown and pitted by rain's incessant yammer.
Plover, willet, swallow, gull dart and hover, scavenge the seasonal
mollusk, bug and brine—that is until this Summer Lake's sudden,
petulant winds scatter the birds to shelter, mischievous gusts conjuring
alkaline dancers—veiled strumpets of dust spinning helter-skelter.

This temporal tarn has no choice but indulge her every mood,
adore her shallow reflection, succumb to each ephemeral whim.
She knows she has little time for the enduring mountains
that brood along her edges, harvesting color and wet
from clouds that provision her evaporating palette; or
for the petering poet who scans the drying alkali flats
and chimeric chorus lines of chalk for too late meaning
and too little rhyme.

Datebook

I carry the new year around for weeks before
it gets here, its smug promise bound in unblemished
black leather, 2017 embossed on the cover, pages edged
with gold leaf and possibility. Inside, unsullied
days plotted three by three as well as, for viewing
convenience, all twelve months on a single page
with tiny phases of the moon waxing over a world
the size of a pin prick.

A white silk ribbon lies slack waiting to mark
something of note, its presence a guarantee
that something will be. In the back, compressed
maps of the world, distended, flat as a halibut,
Holidays and Time Zones, and exactly fourteen
pages for observation and reflection.

On December 31st I hold the virgin year in my palm,
sharpen a pencil to make entries so changes in plan
can be cleanly removed. If I draw my year between
the lines, by next December I will surely be...

Quick Distance

Around her hand she winds the ribbons dangling
from the party balloons—blue and green Mylar moons
and stars, one for each year she is old. She walks
them outside into the cold. They chafe to fly, are filled
with levity, despite the quick distance, the dwindling
years of light. Before releasing the giddy airships,
she inhales the helium, giggles like a fool. One by one
the balloons disappear from sight.

Mutual Creation Society

Today, for example, I decide
the snowflakes that float to the ground
are albino ashes, aftermath of a mute
eruption of an egret volcano.

Those fences? Reduced
to slim theory under the chilly
accumulation of down, the fallen posts
stutterers out of line – dashes
Morse-coding their march across
a snowy infinity.

And those? Crows. Or maybe black
almonds perched on a leafless
limb? I conduct their giggled imitation
of the sadness that whistles
through everyone.

Indoors the haughty violet
amaryllis queen I conjured commands
her fronds to feed her gaudy habit
of ruffled petal, her exposed, spring-like
blossom an affront to the winter outside.

It's perfect. In turn and time, amaryllis
and snow spy me through a lime
or crystal eye and therefore and only then
am I. What I regard is therefore sung
and what sees me offers me as refrain.

Pinhole

Distract me, you say. So I paint the insides
of a shoe box flat black, cut out a square on one
end, cover it with foil, make a tiny pin prick
to let in the thinnest sliver of light, place tape
over the hole, go in the darkroom, place photo
paper inside, roll you out in the sun, aim the foiled
end at you, lift the primitive shutter, count to ten.

Chemicals lift the ghostly image – you
slumped over by sclerosis – down where up, dark
where light should be. You assure me it makes its own
kind of inverted sense...eventually. Strapped
to your wheelchair, you say you are reduced
to seeing life through a pinhole, and it is
still magnificent.

Dream Catcher

I eat standing up because I am about
to be on my way somewhere. I just
know it. I don't sit. The music hasn't
stopped, not yet. And anyway, there's
only one chair and I the only one
here. I line up *Self, Time, Fortune, Vanity
Fair* edge to edge, tuck hospital corners
on the bed, straighten the Oriental rug—
measures of order to tighten the weave,
to increase the chances of a good thing
catching.

What have I already told you?
That life has more meaning
now that I know it doesn't
than when I though it did?
Of course, I love life whenever
I can. Or I will. I swear it. Meanwhile
I'll make sure my fork touches
my plate politely. No haste, clatter,
no shove, no scrape—telling
of one who eats alone.

True Happenings

I

South Wind is the medicine, the magic, the chief here... not coyote, not raven, as on the sere, desert side of these Cascade mountains. Here, by the ocean, it is South Wind, the kelp-robed king, the fooled-you, the transformer. South Wind, with his mossy dreads, his reckless wand. South Wind, with his gale-force tantrums, dreamed between his tree-trunk thighs, pressed low and ocean, then, with a groan, double-fisted ashore. He pushes up from his basaltic throne, orders Thunder Bird, his pope of power, to drum the tempest faster; commands Wild Woman, his ogress accomplice known to eat her own wrinkled history alive, to whip the surf into spit and foam.

Wild Woman. She's a kitchen match, strikes anywhere, that one. Crane, her cuckolded, stilt-legged husband, fords the Salmon River to find her after the storm is over. Splayed on the shore like a starfish, crying from exhaustion, she begs for some consideration. Crane opens his great white wings in what could be a gesture of caring or maybe just to dry them in the wind. These things can be known, but only if you listen to the vespers of spruce, the crackle of the Steller's jay, the thrush's varied whistle, the cheek, cheek of the chorus frog, the pygmy owl's beep, the huff of the musky elk, and the warning caw of the unsated gull.

II

Today that hungry bird circles above me—the great, great granddaughter of the murderers of Native people, language and place, a woman in shorts and sandals who walks the beach after the storm. I pick up small, blue tongues of mussel shell mewing in the tide pools, contemplate their beauty and uselessness, discard them on the sand. The mussels' kin weep, cling to the barnacled black rocks that form an upside-down horseshoe of emptying luck. Who do I think I am to take things out of their ocean's realm, help myself to driftwood, verbs, oysters, ignore the ancient syntax of nouns, flounder, and salmon. Who do I think I am, heiress to an ancestral pox of gunpowder, syphilis and rum. 3,000 Natives lived here in 1800. Thousands more before them. Only 25 left in 1910. And now?

There are not enough words left in their language to describe. Just broken bits of linguistic sea shell: *tla slik, tatag, wac wac.* I bend down again, this time pick up a white rock shaped like a skull. The beach is littered with them, a killing field of sedimented history. They drum their coral fingers while waiting for the overdue subduction, the thrust down deep, the marrow-sucking, ravenous, molten Whale that will put us all, everything, back in our places at the feet of South Wind.

Anaconda Copper

The children arrive in oversized clothes of no particular
color, their eyes crusted from interrupted sleep, to breakfast
at the Headstart Center in the shadow of the naked slopes
of the Anacondas.

After toast and Tang they are lined up for a photograph,
holding their art work under their eyes, large, dark circles
mimicking the place their fathers go every day to mine.

The mothers leave, go to the store. Their forefingers draw
a thick line through the dust on the shelves as they wistfully recall
all the TV had promised, but for the strike. (Their men held out
long as they could, sandwiched between cardboard placards
of protest, before caving in to the copper king.)

They cross the street to gather in Rayleen's living room,
moving the green jar of peacock feathers off the coffee table,
tucking the purple afghan around their feet. They lay out
the supplies: Styrofoam trays saved from packages of ground
chuck, velveteen ordered from a catalogue, and Elmer's glue.

They fashion white stallions rearing, pawing the plush night,
roses with exquisite white Styrofoam petals carefully planted
in a dark velour bed, or ballerinas twirling on a tiny pointed
slipper of foam.

The fathers don't come to the art show.
Just the mothers who hang back against the wall
next to their Styrofoam dreams and their children's
drawings of the black hole in the ground
from which their fathers would never emerge.

American Made

boys' night backyard barbecue,
clay pigeon skeet
"Pull!"
blasted in two.
"Snookered!"
brand new fish cooker.
"Slick smokin' unit, Tom."
Dan pulls up in
decked out Econoline,
vanity plate BZCRUSR.
unloads Ruffles, deli slaw,
case of Coors from red velvet
interior. they beach in lawn chairs
pop a top, swig, belch, one-fisted
crush, backhand empties. lawn studded
with aluminum litter. soiled T's strain
over bellies.
     "Got your bull tag?"
     "Damn straight."
now the jokes.
     "Did ya hear about
     the man offered $2,000 smacks
     if he'd have sex with a gorilla..."
     "As much as I've been gettin'
     I'd do it gratis."
     "Said he'd need some time to raise the money!"
side-splitter.
     "Or did you read how them boys
     north county spotted a Jap-made
     Kawasaki cycle, strung it up
     in a tree, beat it
     to death."
     "Wonder if they raped it first?"
knee slapper.
     "One at a time? Missionary?"
stop, stop
too much
har, hars float in the dusk
mix with the innocent air

it was supposed to be funny

Seiners' Dream

The shores are milky from the milt
of herring. Tiny pearls of translucent roe coat the flat, brown
tongues of ribbon kelp. Planes bank, dip, radio: Go, go! Purse
seiners charge and wheel their million dollar boats in shallow waters,
jockey to set, fill their nets. Buck and flick, charge and lunge!
Herring, herring, eight thousand tons off-loaded.

At the Pioneer Bar later or seated
by the kitchen heater the seiners nibble poppet beads
off seaweed as nimbly as the clicking sperm whale slips
the cod from the long line hook; swallow thin leaves
of smoked salmon with the same gusto as the barking sea
lion gobbles the whole fish.

Boats are moored tight
to the midnight. Houses huddle small against the dark
mountains. The fishermen laugh, pull the wife or waitress
onto their laps, raise glasses of golden beer, "good run,"
"best yet," or "same time next year."

Only in their sleep do they feel the wet,
black strands of the Tlingit herring rock song wrap around their necks;
look inside the insatiable maw of the fish-eating monster; beg
for grace from the stormy chop, the flailing rigging, the looming
peaks of the Tongass that would crowd them into the sea.

Sweet Happenstance

Are we too removed from life
to love, from love
to live? Though we mimic
both, we fear
so much, the nervous one
buttressing the anxious
other, stretched
across an imagined chasm

until that sweet happenstance,
when joy's remembered,
stingy spirit remanded –
this time by a young
girl, roller-skating by,
who, all at once, ricochets
off the sidewalk, glides
on one foot, looks
over her shoulder,
flips her hair,
licks a popsicle,
hops the curb,
and beckons to her friend,
"Come on!"

New Frontier

Miles out to sea from Japan is a giant gyre,
a trash vortex of plastic bigger than Texas,
an island of flip flops, milk jugs, bubble
wrap and grocery sacks.

Plastic ball bearings and packing peanuts line
the arroyos; a shifting Tupperware crust lifts
scarps of prefab shower stalls and mannequin limbs.
In the distance, fields of leached diapers pickle
under the polymer sun.

The island is platted using infra-red lines of plastic light.
Countries fight with plastic guns for the right to rule
this new caliphate, where rivers burn, toxic orange sunsets
are the norm, and tinsel flowers grow from a humus
of polycarbonates.

Higher Still

The pull of Moon returns Tide with his question
to the pages of the shoreline. But because every
arrival is the beginning of leaving (and, as far as
that goes, the promise of return), Tide is no
sooner ashore than he must fold down a barnacled
corner marking where he'll resume his search
for an answer...some muskeg meaning missed,
some pebbly, cavern-dwelling clue to his recent
excesses that eludes this moony poet robed in liquid slate.

Tide strews ribbons of kelp to mark the spot before
any conclusion can be reached about how much
is too much as Moon hurries him away, dooming
this repeating bard to worrying, higher and higher
and higher still, the high-water mark of the world.

For now, Tide recedes as bidden, pushing a sigh through pursed
rock lips, his watery tongue tracing the roof of the breathing cave.

Jump Rope

Cinderella dressed in Double Under! *yellow, went upstairs*
to kiss a fellow. Made a mistake and kissed Criss Cross!
a snake. How many Double Dutch! *doctors did it take?* Go!
High, low, medium, wavy, walkie, talkie, slow, pepper! Recess
done. We all file in. Teacher commands: "Before I count ten.
Under your desks. Duck and cover! Ready when the enemy comes."

I get home and Grandma prattles, "Tomato slammed the door."
The living room smells like low tide. She peed on the divan
again. Grandpa died in an old war. Grandma tries to phone him.
She wears white stockings on her evening stroll, pulls the shades
so the boogey man can't see in, hides her glasses, says
they're lost. I always find them under her mattress.

The maid lives over the kitchen. Her wind-up clock drums
on the bed stand. Jesus bleeds on a white paper doily by a photo
of a man in uniform. "We're her only family, poor thing," says mother.
"She escaped the famine in Ireland." The maid calls me Miss, says
"Good marnin." She holds two boney fingers up to her mouth when
she speaks. I think it's because she's scared.

Today father wants his little soldier to help. He loops a rope round
my chest, hangs me out the window. I prop up the collapsed antenna
so he can get the news. He leaves for weekend army. Mother watches
him go as she pulls hair from my brush. The blonde tuft drifts toward
the ocean like a sad ending. What's a bomb shelter? She just says,
"Don't go near the public pool." Polio. I learn in school some mushrooms
can kill you. And there are clouds like those mushrooms.

Grandma pinches the skin on the top of her hand, I pinch mine. Hers stays
tented for eons. She says: "Time and tide wait for no man." I run
to the shore. *One two three O'Leary, eight, nine, ten O'Leary.* I jump every
wave and white cap, boat and buoy. *Teddy bear, teddy bear go upstairs.* I skip
rope every boy I want to kiss. Jump the new sneakers with navy blue trim.
The poplin bedspread for my room. *Teddy bear, teddy bear, say your prayers.*
I jump and jump. *What time is it Mr. Wolf, Mr. Wolf? What time is it?*

The Next to Last Question

"What is our work in a wounded world?"

KATHLEEN DEAN MOORE, ENVIRONMENTAL ACTIVIST AND AUTHOR

It's no longer hope that gets me
up in the morning, but the alarm
that sounds.

Do Eskimos have a right
to ice? Will my grandsons live
under glacial melt?

Does my pleasure
in this groaning board
depend on my ignorance?

What if I say, from now on,
I'll call it,
by its right name,
choose carefully
what I do each day?

The answer can't be
postponed
with more questions.

So then, here is my tilth.
With words for seeds
I'll choose a plot of desert
and write it, write it,
back to health.

DEC 2 0 2017

CPSIA information can be obtained
at www.ICGtesting.com
Printed in the USA
LVOW10s1303241117
557360LV00014B/1038/P